Is It Something I Said?

A Play

Richard Harris

A SAMUEL FRENCH ACTING EDITION

SAMUEL FRENCH

FOUNDED 1830

SAMUELFRENCH-LONDON.CO.UK
SAMUELFRENCH.COM

CHARACTERS

Wallace
Arthur
Stella

The action takes place in a seedy hotel near Paddington
Station

Time—the present

IS IT SOMETHING I SAID?

*A third-rate hotel near Paddington Station. Early November.
Evening*

*To one side there is a small reception area, represented as simply as
possible—a counter with a register book, perhaps a key-rack. Next
to the reception area, and directly facing the audience, there is a
simple wall with painted doors and a notice (of seeming permanence)
which announces "Lift Out Of Order". On the other side of this
wall, there is a narrow space to represent an upstairs corridor and a
door leading into the third-floor bedroom, on the other side of the
stage*

*A most depressing bedroom. A single bed, a small table and chair, a
gas fire with meter, a washbasin with dripping tap, a window with
curtains on a heavy rail. On the wall over the bed, there is an
intercom: a plastic box clearly wired up by an amateur enthusiast*

When the CURTAIN *rises, the slow clank-clank of a passing goods
train is heard. The action will be punctuated throughout by railway
noises, including perhaps the sound of an approaching and slowing
Inter-City express*

*Wallace is filling in the register. A nondescript man of about fifty,
with a suitcase at his feet. He is being studiously watched across the
counter by Arthur. A man much the same as Wallace, he runs this
place with his wife. As Wallace writes, he whistles cheerfully and
tunelessly under his breath. This tuneless humming punctuates all
the earlier exchanges*

*A moment, as Wallace does his careful longhand and Arthur studies
him*

Arthur Were you recommended?
Wallace Sorry?
Arthur Are you here as the result of a recommendation?
Wallace No, no—purely on the off-chance. In passing as it were.
(*He resumes his humming for a moment and then smiles and holds
out the biro for Arthur*) There. All done.

Arthur pockets the biro and turns the book round to read

Arthur "Leslie William Wallace, number eighty-four Park View Crescent West, Croydon." What's this? Oh, I see . . . you've included your telephone number.

Wallace Have I? Oh yes so I have. Might I have the key to my room?

Arthur (*producing the key*) I'll show you up: it's number thirty-three.

Wallace Aha! (*He beams, and resumes humming*)

Arthur moves out from behind the desk, takes up the suitcase and exits behind the lift wall

Wallace cups his hands behind his back and follows Arthur dutifully

A moment

Stella enters the reception area, behind the counter

In her mid-forties, she is tight-faced with lips set in a permanent prune of disapproval. She is wearing a flowered housecoat with matching headscarf beneath which is the hint of a hair curler, and a pair of yellow rubber gloves. She enters slowly, and clearly in pain from her terrible migraine, but seeing the place is empty, she perks herself up miraculously

Stella Arthur? *Arthur?* (*She shakes her head, the mouth forming into an even-tighter prune*) How I carry on against all odds like this, I do not know, I really do not know.

And she reaches under the counter to produce a large digestive biscuit which she nibbles as she exits

Arthur and Wallace enter from the other side of the lift wall. Arthur is puffing somewhat, Wallace is looking around brightly, still humming

Arthur We do have a lift of course but unfortunately it was vandalized in celebration of the Scottish victory at Wembley last whatsit.

Wallace I don't understand these people, truly I don't.

Arthur I'm often at a loss myself. Good as gold they were before kick-off. I remember saying to my wife . . . "What a nice class of supporter they've brought down this year. Twenty-four hours later and there's our lift poised between the second and third like a gaping wound. Anyway . . . you'll enjoy number thirty-three, I've just had it re-decorated.

He unlocks the door, turns on the light and stands aside to let Wallace through. They enter. Wallace stands, taking in the room. His humming has become that little bit more manic. Arthur crosses the room to put the key on the table and the suitcase on the floor

Wallace Oh yes. Very—er—pleasant. Very pleasant indeed.

Arthur crosses to switch off the dripping tap. He can't stop it so he changes the subject by crossing to the bed and bouncing the corner with his hand

Arthur Brand-new, that mattress. Interior sprung, both ways. Sleep like the dead.

Wallace stops humming instantly

Wallace I notice there's a gas fire.
Arthur We try to make the rooms as cosy as poss—some of these places you go to . . .
Wallace That looks useful. (*He indicates the plastic box over the bed*)
Arthur (*moving to it and indicating*) This is part of the inter-communication system.
Wallace Well there we are, you see—I could tell it was useful as soon as I saw it.
Arthur Should you require anything—that is, until eleven o'clock p.m.—up with the switch, direct contact with reception.
Wallace Aha!
Arthur *Will* you be requiring anything, do you think?

He looks somewhat challengingly at Wallace who stares back for a moment

Wallace The thing is, I don't want to be disturbed. I've had a very long day. I've been travelling, you see. From Cornwall. South Cornwall. This is by way of being an overnight stop before I continue my journey. Up North. Newcastle upon Tyne. And possibly even more so. As soon as you're out of this room I shall be into that bed and fast asleep.

Arthur And there's me keeping you chatting.
Wallace Normally I enjoy a good conversation.
Arthur I can see that.
Wallace I'll bid you good-night then.
Arthur I shall personally see to it that you are not disturbed. (*He moves to the door*)
Wallace On the other hand . . .
Arthur Yes?

A moment. And Wallace finally comes up with

Wallace A glass of hot milk would be most acceptable.
Arthur Milk.
Wallace And—er—here's a pound note. I would like some change for the gas.
Arthur For the gas.
Wallace What coins does it take?
Arthur Fivepenny pieces.
Wallace So that's five into—that's twenty—no, forty—no, twenty—yes—I'll have twenty fivepenny pieces if you would be so kind.
Arthur Twenty.
Wallace *Si vous voulez.*
Arthur That's a glass of hot milk and twenty fivepenny pieces.
Wallace *Oui.*
Arthur Right. I'll bring it up.
Wallace There's no——

But Arthur is already gone and closing the door behind him
   —hurry.

   Arthur exits behind the wall

Wallace stands for a moment. He sighs, then goes to draw the curtains. He turns and looks down at the gas fire, then takes up the suitcase, puts it on the bed and opens it. He takes out a pen, writing paper and envelopes, sits at the table and begins writing

   Arthur enters the reception area carrying a tin tray on which is a saucer. He reaches under the counter to produce a pint of milk

   Stella enters

Stella You're not stuffing yourself again, I trust?

Arthur No, my dear. I'm preparing a glass of hot milk for our
  new guest.
Stella Oh yes? When did *he* arrive?
Arthur Just——
Stella Why didn't you say? You know I like to give our guests a
  personal welcome.
Arthur You were lying down with your migraine.
Stella I would have *risen*.
Arthur Anyway . . . it seems to have passed over.
Stella Don't make light of my suffering, Arthur, it doesn't
  become you.
Arthur No my dear. Will you be going out this evening?
Stella I shall take a bath and see how I feel . . . (*She starts to go*)
  And don't use a mug, Arthur—not for the guests. Put it in the
  blue . . . the nice new blue.

  Stella exits

Arthur Certainly my dear. The blue . . . the nice new blue . . .

  He exits behind the wall with the tray and bottle of milk

Wallace is composing a letter with some difficulty

Wallace "Dear . . . Irene . . . I cannot go on and have therefore
  decided to end it. All. End it all." (*He stares at the pad. Then
  rips out the page and screws it into a ball angrily. He sighs,
  feeling very sorry for himself. The sight of the intercom box
  gives him an idea. He crosses and presses the switch*)

The intercom buzzes in the reception area

  *As it does so, Arthur enters with the tray, which now holds a
  rather nasty blue cup and saucer and a pile of coins. He bends
  low and appears to be speaking to the counter top*

Arthur Reception.
Wallace Umm . . . this is—er—Mr Wallace in room—er . . .
Arthur Thirty-three.
Wallace Yes, room thirty-three. I wonder if I might—er—bother
  you for—er—a little something to eat.
Arthur What had you in mind?
Wallace Oh, just a little peccadillo.
Arthur In what shape?

Wallace Umm . . . something like a biscuit?
Arthur (*after frowning*) I'll bring one up with the milk and the
    fivepenny pieces.
Wallace Thank you so much. (*He moves back to the table, sits and
    begins another letter*)

*Arthur considers a moment, then reaches under the counter to bring
out a battered biscuit tin from which he takes four biscuits. He puts
them in the saucer, changes his mind and puts two back in the tin*

    He exits behind the wall with the tray

"My dearest Irene . . . this is the only way out. Please understand . . . and forgive me . . . if I cause you pain . . ." No.
". . . for the pain I am causing you." No. ". . . you and the
children." Er . . . no. ". . . causing *you*. Your ever-loving
Leslie." (*He tears off the page, puts it in an envelope, licks it
down, sits a moment, then props the letter up against a large
ashtray in the centre of the table. Dissatisfied, he rearranges it,
propping it up again*)

Arthur puffs into sight, knocks at the door

One moment please!

*A final adjustment of the envelope and he crosses to open the door to
Arthur who comes in*

Arthur I managed a couple of digestives.
Wallace You're very kind.
Arthur (*pointing to the tray*) Milk . . . and twenty . . . fivepenny
    pieces.
Wallace I wonder if you'd be so kind as to put the tray *sur la
    table*?
Arthur Eh? Oh, certainly, certainly . . .
Wallace I'll just move this letter—make it easier for you.

Arthur puts the tray down on the table and makes for the door

The thing is——

Arthur turns

—I've just written a letter. To my wife. More of a note, really.
Yes. Ummm . . . what I was going to say is . . . should I happen

to forget it tomorrow—that is, in my haste—I was wondering if you could make sure she gets it. Personally. She'll be wondering where I *am*, you see.

A slight pause. If Wallace was hoping for some form of enquiry from Arthur, none is coming

Arthur Yes.

> *Arthur goes out, closing the door behind him, and exits behind the wall*

Wallace sighs, takes up the cup of milk and sips it. Then he sees the piles of coins and takes them up. He goes to the gas fire. A moment. Then he bends and starts feeding all the coins into the meter

> *At the same time, Arthur enters the reception area carrying a large mug of tea. He sips it*

> *Stella enters. She still wears the housecoat, but has her hair done and her face made up rather too much. She is waving her hands about to dry her nail varnish*

Stella You're not drinking more tea, are you? And the colour of it . . . how many spoonfuls do you put in, I dread to think of the state of your stomach I do, I really do. And don't leave that pot on the reception counter, Arthur . . . it's 'ardly a work of art, 'ardly conclusive to good public relations now is it? Anyway . . . I *shall* be popping out . . . just for half an hour or so.

Arthur Oh yes my dear?

Stella Don't say it like that, Arthur. If I don't get my little break from the wear and tear of this establishment I shall have a breakdown, I know I will. And I shall be needing the car, where have you put the keys?

Arthur They'll be in your bag—the crocodile—you took the car last night if you remember.

Stella I don't think I like your tone of voice, Arthur.

In the bedroom, Wallace goes to his suitcase and takes out a large roll of Sellotape and a large pair of scissors

Arthur I was simply trying to point out——

Stella It is quite clear, Arthur, that as far as you are concerned, life is nothing but a bowl of innuendoes. I sometimes wonder what goes on in that head of yours, I do. I really do.

She exits, more concerned with her nails

Arthur leans on the counter, thoughtfully sipping tea and staring straight ahead

Wallace takes the chair to the door, stands on it, and proceeds to stick Sellotape all round the door. He takes the key from the table, locks the door, removes the key and puts a criss-cross of tape across the keyhole. He stands back and admires his work. He is suddenly exhausted, and slumps into the chair and stares at the door

Stella enters the reception area, done up to the nines

Arthur is studying a greenhouse brochure he has taken from under the counter

Stella You'll be all right then, will you heart?
Arthur You won't be long, will you?
Stella I've *said*. If number seventeen gets up to his tricks again, tell him he'll have me to answer to.
Arthur What time do I expect you then?
Stella Don't fuss, Arthur, don't *shackle* me. If it looks like I shall be detained I'll give you a tinkle. What's that you're reading?
Arthur One of my brochures.
Stella I wish you wouldn't read brochures, Arthur—you know how it unsettles your system.

Stella exits

Throughout the above, Wallace has remained seated, staring. Now he stands, mentally making a note, his lips moving soundlessly—money in the meter, letter to Irene, door. He moves slowly across to the gas fire and looks down at it. With the supreme moment of determination, he quickly bends down and turns on the gas tap. Or would turn it on, but it's stuck

Arthur peruses his brochure as Wallace heaves at the tap. His hand slips. He rams it in his mouth so that he can scream soundlessly, then he dances up and down on the spot, waving the offended hand, almost in tears

Wallace Damn rotten thing . . . damn *rotten* thing. (*He hurries across and switches on the intercom*)

The intercom buzzes in the reception area. Arthur frowns and bends low to speak

Arthur Reception.
Wallace Er . . . this is Mr Wallace in room thirty-three.
Arthur Oh yes?
Wallace I wonder if you would be so kind as to spare me a minute.
Arthur You mean come up?
Wallace Er . . . yes.
Arthur Is something wrong?
Wallace Er . . . I'd rather not discuss it on the—er—the thing.

A moment

Arthur I'll come up then.

He frowns, then hurriedly exits behind the lift wall

Wallace paces, taking out his handkerchief to wrap it round his injured hand

Arthur enters, puffing heavily, having run up the stairs. He knocks on the door

Wallace Who's that?
Arthur Me.
Wallace Oh. One moment please. (*He makes to answer the door, realizes it is taped up, and starts to rip off the tape*)

Arthur, still puffing, puts his ear to the door, listening to the sounds of the tape being ripped off, and Wallace's grunts of exertion. Wallace finishes, fetches the key and unlocks the door. He opens it and indicates—with tape-wrapped hands—that Arthur should come in. He does so. Wallace moves away and discreetly gets the sticky tape from his hands. Arthur stands by the door, taking in the scene

(*Cheerfully*) The thing is . . . the gas doesn't work.
Arthur (*eyes to the fire*) The gas?
Wallace Yes. I was lying down—that is, I was about to lie down —when I felt a bit chilly.
Arthur The tap's stuck.

Wallace So I discovered. (*He indicates his damaged hand and manages a little laugh*)

Arthur (*more to himself*) I should have put you in number twenty-seven.

Wallace Should have what?

Arthur I say I can move you into number twenty-seven.

Wallace It works in number twenty-seven, does it?

Arthur A guaranteed one hundred per cent flow.

Wallace Ah. Excuse me . . . (*He moves past Arthur and pointedly removes a piece of tape from the door*) I don't think a move will be necessary, thank you. I just wanted you to know that I tried to turn on the gas and it didn't work. I just wanted you to know that. (*He looks hard at Arthur but gets nothing like the response he was hoping for*) Should your future clientele—wish to make use of it. I just wanted to make it clear—*absolument* clear—that I did try and it didn't work. I did *try*. (*He takes up the roll of Sellotape and the scissors, puts them in the suitcase, closes the lid, turns and beams at Arthur*)

Arthur It would work in number twenty-seven.

Wallace Yes. That reminds me. I heard this joke yesterday. Did you hear about the Scotsman who was so mean he broke into the house next door to gas himself?

Arthur No.

Wallace Yes. The point being, of course, to show just how far a human being will sink when he's at the end of his tether. Even a Scotsman.

Arthur I wouldn't have said gas was a very good idea, myself. No. People smell gas, don't they? Raise the alarm. Gas can creep. Through gaps. Round the door, for example.

Wallace I'm not saying he succeeded, this Scotsman—all I'm saying is that at least he tried.

Arthur He would have done a lot better in number twenty-seven: no-one ever goes down that end of the corridor.

Wallace (*increasingly irritable*) He could still have been talked *out* of it.

Arthur On the other hand, there would seem very little point of going *into* it.

Wallace Why is that, *pourquoi*?

Arthur Because we have been converted. And natural gas is not what they call toxical. All he would have got, this Scotch friend

of yours, is a nasty headache. (*Going*) I'll leave you to it then.
Wallace Before you go——

Arthur stops

——this is the third floor, *n'est-ce-pas*?
Arthur Third floor, yes.
Wallace Might I ask what is outside that window?
Arthur A sheer drop.
Wallace Leading where?
Arthur In what way?
Wallace As the crow flies—always assuming of course that this
  particular crow has given up the effort.
Arthur In that case it would find itself plummeting towards a
  solid concrete area surrounded by metal pailings.
Wallace With very little chance of survival?
Arthur None at all.
Wallace Just a heap of mincemeat and feathers.
Arthur See for yourself. (*He moves and tries to raise the window
  but it won't budge*)
Wallace (*smugly*) It seems to be stuck.
Arthur It's those painters . . . if there's one thing I cannot stand
  it's shoddy workmanship.
Wallace I might say that I was hoping to look out of that window
  . . . to get a breath of fresh air before turning in.
Arthur I'll fetch my hammer—loosen it up a bit.
Wallace I would of course have to be very careful and not lean
  out too far—suffering as I do from heavy vertigo.
Arthur Let me fetch my hammer. (*He hurries towards the door*)
Wallace I've changed my mind.
Arthur Two minutes.
Wallace What I would really like is a piece of rope.
Arthur What had you in mind?
Wallace I want to tie up my suitcase.
Arthur I might manage a piece of flex.
Wallace Something about this long . . . (*he indicates arms' width*)
  . . . big enough to tie a knot in.
Arthur I'll have a look in my toolbox.
Wallace Yes, flex might do the trick . . . heavy-duty flex of
  course. They say it's very strong, flex. They *say* that if you were
  to tie it up somewhere . . . say that curtain rail . . . and hang a

heavy weight on the other end ... say something about my size ... heavy-duty electrical flex would stand the strain with no trouble at all.

Arthur Just the job.

Wallace In that case, forget the hammer, I'll settle for the flex.

Arthur Right.

Wallace On the other hand, what about the rail? We know about the flex, but would that rail stand the strain?

Arthur That rail is fixed by six four-inch number twelves. I installed it myself. That rail would support a horse.

Wallace (*moving closer to Arthur*) So what you are saying is, that if a horse were suspended from that rail by a length of heavy-duty electrical flex, it could do so with a certain amount of grace and with little fear of that rail collapsing and breaking its *neck*.

Arthur No chance.

Wallace That horse could dangle there all night, without fear of breaking its neck and without fear of being disturbed.

Arthur I would personally guarantee it.

Wallace Would your guarantee hold good if *I* decided to suspend myself from that rail and forgot about the horse?

Arthur I don't think I heard that.

Wallace I'll rephrase it then: I am going to kill myself.

Arthur Yes.

Wallace Is that *it*? "Yes."

Arthur I mean ... oh yes?

Wallace (*menacingly*) "Oh yes?" "Oh *yes*?" Where's your sense of duty?

Arthur (*affronted*) I made you a cup of hot milk.

Wallace You have a duty to save my life.

Arthur Why?

Wallace Eh?

Arthur *Why?*

Wallace Because people *do*.

Arthur I've never met you before.

Wallace What's that got to do with it?

Arthur A perfect stranger interfering with your personal decisions—it's not on.

Wallace People get *medals*.

Arthur Interfering people.

Wallace Heroes.

Arthur I did my bit during the war.

Wallace You've known all along, haven't you? You knew as soon as I walked in this place.

Arthur Well whose fault was that?

Wallace Whose fault?

Arthur You book in—you put your full name and address *and* your phone number—I'm surprised you didn't put your next-of-kin and be done with it . . . then you pay in advance and when I offer early-morning tea you refuse it. No-one refuses early-morning tea. It's one of the joys.

The wind is leaving Wallace's sails

Wallace I haven't done this sort of thing before.

Arthur You should have done a bit of *research*—found out. They *always* pay in advance—leave the house in order you might say—minimize the problems of the bereaved. I mean, can you imagine me going up to your wife and saying "Excuse me Mrs Wallace, your hubbie's just done himself in and can I have six pound seventy-five for the room?" Carry on like that and I'd be bankrupt. That you *did* pay in advance is a question of human nature and nothing to do with research. It's like throwing yourself under a train—you don't buy a return ticket because you won't be needing it. That's human *nature*. You should have researched that in order to throw me off the scent, left the bill till the morning, ordered your tea. The *Daily Express*. Left your shoes out. I try to close my eyes—let you get on with it—and what do I get? Abuse.

Wallace finds himself listening with growing sympathy to Arthur's problem

Wallace I really am very sorry. I should have thought.

Arthur If only you people would *think*. That's all. (*He sighs*)

A moment

Wallace I still say that having found out, you should have prevented it.

Arthur Who am I to tell you what to do with your life?

Wallace It's my death I'm talking about.

Arthur It's bound to happen sooner or later. The only thing you can bank on in life is death.

Wallace There's no need to be morbid.

Arthur Life is like being on a train. Sooner or later we all have to get off. You happen to have chosen to get off three stops early, that's all.

Wallace Yes, but I could have changed my mind. I might have done it and found out I didn't fancy it after all.

Arthur How do you know you won't walk out of here, go down the station and fall under the very train you're supposed to be travelling on?

Wallace You're talking about an accident.

Arthur Exactly: what *you* have done is come to a decision. Eliminated the unforeseen. It's not my fault you chose to do it in a room where the gas doesn't work. I had you chalked down as a pills man.

Wallace I *never* take pills.

Arthur I'm *sorry:* I made a *mistake.*

Wallace I could have prevented all this if she'd packed my razor.

Arthur The wife?

Wallace Can't rely on her to do anything.

Arthur Typical. (*He gives a scornful little jerk of the head*)

Wallace I didn't mean to be offensive.

Arthur I can see you're very depressed.

Wallace There doesn't seem much point in going on.

Arthur Let me see if I can get that window open.

Wallace I didn't really fancy it, to tell the truth.

Arthur Bit messy I must say.

Wallace I've always been so fastidious: well, known for it, really.

Arthur Still: don't give up hope. Try and look on the dark side, see if you can work yourself into something.

Wallace I'm a bit confused.

Arthur You'd made up your mind on the gas.

Wallace I put twenty fivepenny pieces in that meter.

Arthur I know: I had to go round the off-licence to get 'em.

Wallace Oh—sorry.

Arthur No, no.

Wallace Incidentally, two of them were Irish.

Arthur I'll speak to him about that: good job you noticed.

Wallace I was just glancing through them for something to read, really.

Arthur You should've said: I would have brought up a magazine.

Wallace Skinned my knuckles something terrible trying to get that tap open.

He shows Arthur the hand. Arthur sucks in air

Arthur You want to look after that.
Wallace And it was the wrong gas anyway.
Arthur Still—you can't think of *everything*, can you?

Wallace sighs heavily, slumps into the chair

That's the—er—that's the note, is it?
Wallace To the wife.
Arthur Might I?

Wallace gestures vaguely towards the letter. Arthur opens it, reads, shaking his head slightly

Mmmm.
Wallace No good?
Arthur Typical really. I mean, you take this bit: "This is the only way out." That's what they all say. Typical.
Wallace Well . . . it's how I felt at the time.
Arthur What I mean is . . . way out of what?
Wallace My problems.
Arthur Money?
Wallace Income tax. It's murder for the small trader nowadays.
Arthur That's your reason, is it?
Wallace I can't go on.
Arthur I see.

He returns the letter. The tone of his "I see" brings Wallace to

Wallace What d'you mean—"I see"?
Arthur No, no . . .
Wallace What are you implying?
Arthur Far be it——
Wallace I don't like your tone.
Arthur If you think that's why you're killing yourself, that's good enough.
Wallace I *know* that's why I'm killing myself. It's me who's doing it, you know.
Arthur All I'm saying is . . . that if everyone who had trouble with the taxman did away with himself, the government could go

into the funeral business. More than likely it'd be the only department to make a profit. I think you might be on to something: consider the possibilities . . . the Ministry of Labour gets you a job . . . then when you're over the hill the tax man puts on the pressure, you do yourself in, and the government fixes you up with a state funeral. Well, a funeral on the state. In that way they could control the labour force of the country and minimize the outlay on pensions something rotten.

Wallace I'm not doing it for my country, you know—I've got problems of my own.

Arthur Financial problems.

Wallace It's a fact.

Arthur It's a cover-up.

Wallace For what?

Arthur For what is known as the awful reality of your situation. Still. You know best.

Wallace No, come on, come on . . .

Arthur I've said—it's not for me to interfere in your personal decisions . . .

Wallace I'm asking you.

Arthur You've obviously been blotting it out for years.

Wallace Blotting what out?

Arthur Well . . . your wife for a start.

Wallace I love my wife.

Arthur That I don't doubt: but does she love you?

Wallace She thinks the world of me.

Arthur She didn't pack your razor.

Wallace She had other things on her mind.

Arthur Such as what?

Wallace Such as . . . her needlework classes.

Arthur Goes to evening classes, does she?

Wallace Three times a week. Got a very lively mind, my wife.

Arthur So three times a week you go without your dinner.

Wallace I don't mind.

Arthur Ah! You say you don't mind . . . but inside . . . *inside*.

Wallace I like her going to evening classes. I went myself once. *Français*. Common Market. Et cetera.

Arthur As long as you're sure that's where she goes.

Wallace Of course she goes.

Arthur Have you seen her then?

Wallace I don't have to see her.
Arthur So you've only got her word for it.
Wallace (*unsure now*) I trust her.
Arthur Of course you trust her. We all trust her. But we don't know, do we? We don't *know*. Got her own car, has she?
Wallace *She* cleans it.
Arthur She could be out there now ... driving around ... laughing and joking ... and where do you enter into her philosophy? Nowhere. No-*where*. She should be here ... at home ... giving you a decent hot dinner, helping you run the rotten business ... instead of which, you're stuck here, working yourself to the bone, running up and down those lousy stairs while she's sipping sherry with that flash-Harry of a furniture representative.
Wallace (*off on his own track*) Where's her samples?
Arthur What happened to all those dreams?
Wallace She used to bring home samples of her handiwork.
Arthur A man's entitled to his dreams.
Wallace The past few weeks—nothing. What's going on?
Arthur Deliberately flaunting it in your face.
Wallace I knew it ... I knew it.

Each has been off on his own track. Now they come together again

Arthur When was the last time she slept in the marital bed?
Wallace She always sleeps there.
Arthur Hair in curlers—pair of your Viyella pyjamas.
Wallace I wouldn't know: I sleep in the spare room.
Arthur Ever since she was struck down with the migraine.
Wallace Her back. She has trouble with her back.
Arthur And what do *you* have?
Wallace Nothing.
Arthur Women.
Wallace I hate her ... I hate her.
Arthur We *all* do.
Wallace It's not just her—I could put up with her—it's the kids.
Arthur Never talk to you.
Wallace Treat me like dirt.
Arthur Their own father.
Wallace I walk into a room and they walk out.

Arthur You work and slave to give 'em a decent education and when they've got it you're not good enough for 'em.

Wallace They'll be gone soon: lives of their own.

Arthur Dropping in, once a month, Sunday tea, like they're doing you some big favour.

Wallace At least there'll be some sort of conversation. The rest of the time, just me and her.

Arthur It doesn't bear thinking about.

Wallace Kill myself? I wouldn't give her the satisfaction.

Arthur When did she ever give you any?

Wallace And there's me blaming it all on the Inland Revenue.

A moment

Arthur Mind you . . . you *are* a failure. I mean, I wouldn't like you to get the wrong idea. I wasn't trying to stop you killing yourself . . . all I wanted to do was make quite sure you're doing it for the right reasons.

Wallace (*all he can manage*) Oh yes?

Arthur It's all very well blaming the family but what is loud and clear is that they've got no respect for you. What you must ask yourself is "Why haven't they?" Respect is something you earn. By personality. By achievement. What have *you* achieved? I would say—just from hearing you talk—that if a man is measured by his achievements, you go about a pound and a quarter. I mean, you can't even do a decent job of putting yourself out of your misery. You don't mind me talking like this, do you? You do understand that I'm just trying to be helpful.

Wallace (*somewhat bewildered*) Thank you.

Arthur What it all comes down to is personality defects. Take for example your reasons for choosing this hotel. Why choose this hotel?

Wallace Well . . . it seemed as good as any . . .

Arthur What I'm getting at is—why not do it at home?

Wallace I was thinking of the wife.

Arthur Coming home after her evening classes-ho-ho and find-ing you.

Wallace I've always tried to be considerate.

Arthur Didn't matter about me though—you were quite prepared for me to find you.

Wallace Well I had to do it *somewhere*.

Arthur So why not in the comfort of your own home? *You* say it was consideration for your good lady. *I* say it was self-pity. "Poor old Les . . . why did he have to do it *there*? A second-rate hotel in Paddington. He didn't want to upset the wife. Trust old Les, thoughtful to the end."

Wallace Whose side are you on?

Arthur There could of course be another reason. A hotel means people and people means a chance of being discovered. Saved in the nick of time you might say. Where's your determination? Where's your pride? No wonder they've got no respect for you.

Wallace I had every intention of . . .

Arthur You take that Colonel What's-his-name in number eighteen. One of our residents. Seventy-four years old and unable to move a step without the use of about fifteen ton of aluminium scaffolding. That man used to play scrum-half for the Saracens . . . leader of men he was—he's still got the moustache for it. All those years fighting for his country, all those years bringing up a family—and who cares tuppence for him now? Cries himself to sleep every night on a mixture of Irish whiskey and lager. I said to him, last New Year's Eve . . . "What is the point of going on," I said. "What is the *point*?" And all he does is shake my hand and tell me what a lovely fellah I am. You just can't *help* these people.

Wallace (*in deep gloom now*) What would you suggest?

Arthur Do away with yourself by all means, but make it a bit harder on her.

Wallace The wife?

Arthur Make the cow suffer. Now—is there anyone you detest—outside your immediate nearest and dearest of course.

Wallace Only Kenwright.

Arthur Who's he?

Wallace The tax inspector.

Arthur Perfect. It's just a matter of re-writing that note. Something like . . . "My dear Irene . . . I have found out about you and Mr Kenwright. I am doing the noble thing. Yours sincerely, Les." How does that sound?

Wallace To be honest, a bit spiteful. I mean he's only doing his job.

Arthur All right—try this. You write another note, using a

heavily-disguised handwriting and signing off with an unusual
signature. L. W. Wallace. William. Willy. Something like that.
Then you do away with yourself in a way that could suggest
foul play. Think of it . . . all those coppers . . . post-mortem . . .
ruthless interrogation of nearest and dearest . . . skeletons pro-
truding from every conceivable cupboard . . . you could be the
centre of her misery for *months*.

Wallace She'd never forgive me.

Arthur That's the beauty of it. Les the suicide . . . ten a penny . . .
but Les the *murder* victim . . . mystery, hidden depths . . . all
there for the taking.

A moment

Wallace I'll do it.

Arthur I knew it!

Wallace Only not here. (*He locks his suitcase*)

Arthur Waddya mean—not here?

Wallace I'll do it—but not here. It wouldn't be fair, you're quite
right. I'm too considerate. I couldn't involve you, you've been
too helpful—no, it wouldn't be right.

Arthur You can't walk out of here just like that.

Wallace I owe it to you—as a friend.

Arthur But no-one *ever* commits suicide here. They come through
that door, full of good intentions, but they never *do* it. What's
wrong with these people?

Wallace takes Arthur's hand and shakes it

Wallace I expect you'll be reading about me in the local paper.

Arthur I'm *always* reading about it in the local paper. They go
down like ninepins. Foreigners even. They come over here for
the specific purpose . . . but not once have they done it in *my
hotel*. It's not as if I'm not amenable . . . (*He grabs Wallace's
lapels*) Am I or am I not amenable?

Wallace (*freeing himself*) Anyway, thanks very much. I've got to
admit, when I came here, I wasn't sure. If it hadn't been for
you, I would never have made up my mind. (*He moves to the
door with his case*) I *will*. Yes. *Absolument*.

*He goes out, resuming his inane humming, and exits behind the
lift wall*

Arthur remains staring after him

Stella enters the reception area. She checks her lipstick and straightens her blouse

Stella Arthur? (*She bends and presses the unseen intercom*)

The intercom buzzes in the bedroom

Are you there, Arthur?

Arthur slowly turns to stare with hatred at the box. Then he moves across and answers it

Arthur You've come back then, have you my dear?
Stella I've been ringing all over for you . . .

Wallace enters quickly

Stella's attitude changes. Arthur stares at the box: he can hear the following exchange

Goodbye, sir, have a pleasant journey.
Wallace Thank you so much.
Stella Going somewhere nice?
Wallace I'm going to kill myself.
Stella Oh well, as long as you enjoy yourself, I always say.
Wallace *Au revoir.*
Stella *Merci.*
Wallace (*as he exits*) I will do it, I promise you.

Wallace exits

Stella (*speaking into the intercom*) What are you *doing* up there?
Arthur (*flatly*) I'm thinking about killing myself.
Stella That'll be the day. Come down here and get these books sorted out, my head is bursting, truly bursting it is. Are you *listening*, Arthur?
Arthur Yes dearest. I'm listening.

They both switch off their intercoms, both looking ahead. Arthur stares into space, Stella puts fresh lipstick on to her vulgar prune of a mouth

If only one'll do it . . . just one . . . and then I'll do it.

A moment. And then he makes a sudden hand movement across his throat in a cutting motion

I will!

He resumes staring. Outside, a train clanks slowly by. The Lights fade as——

the CURTAIN *falls*

FURNITURE AND PROPERTY LIST

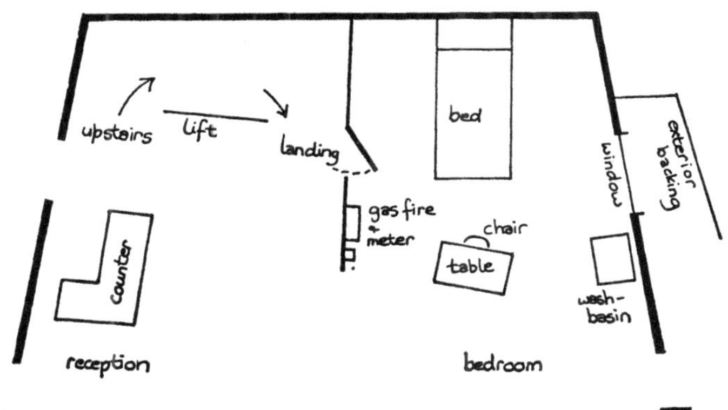

On Stage:	*Reception Area:*
	Counter. *On it:* register, pen. *Behind it:* key rack and keys. *Under it:* tin of digestive biscuits, pint of milk, greenhouse brochure, lipstick
	Notice on lift doors: "LIFT OUT OF ORDER"
	Wallace's suitcase. *In it:* writing paper, envelopes, pen, roll of Sellotape, scissors
	Bedroom:
	Single bed with bedding
	Small table. *On it:* ashtray
	Chair
	Gas fire and meter
	Washbasin and taps (one permanently dripping)
	Curtains on heavy rail
	On wall above bed: intercom
Off stage:	Saucer on tin tray (**Arthur**)
	Blue cup and pile of fivepenny pieces (**Arthur**)
	Large mug of tea (**Arthur**)
Personal:	**Wallace:** £1 note, handkerchief

LIGHTING PLOT

Practical fittings required: pendant in bedroom

Interior. A reception area, a landing, a bedroom. The same scene
throughout

To open: Reception area and landing lit

Cue 1   **Arthur** switches on main light in bedroom   **(Page 3)**
Snap on pendant in bedroom

Cue 2   **Arthur:** "I will!" (*He resumes staring*)   **(Page 22)**
Slow fade to Black-out

EFFECTS PLOT

Throughout the play, there should be railway noises in the background, ranging from the slow clank-clank of goods trains to the sound of an approaching and slowing Inter-City express. Cues are given for those train noises specifically mentiond in the text

Cue 1	As CURTAIN rises *Slow clank of passing goods train*	(Page 1)
Cue 2	**Wallace** presses intercom *Buzz in reception area*	(Page 5)
Cue 3	**Wallace** presses intercom *Buzz in reception area*	(Page 9)
Cue 4	**Stella** bends towards counter to press unseen intercom *Buzz in bedroom*	(Page 21)
Cue 5	**Arthur:** "I will!" (*He resumes staring*) *Slow clank of passing train*	(Page 22)

MADE AND PRINTED IN GREAT BRITAIN BY
LATIMER TREND & COMPANY LTD PLYMOUTH

MADE IN ENGLAND